Banjo Picking Tunes

AN EARLY AMERICAN CHRISTMAS

by Lluís Gómez

Online Audio

To access the online audio recording go to:
WWW.MELBAY.COM/30910MEB

The Prucha Spirit Jason Burleson Signature Model banjo cover image courtesy of Prucha Bluegrass Instruments.

WWW.MELBAY.COM

Preface

The joyous Christmas season has inspired musicians in many countries and in many eras to compose beautiful songs. This book contains 17 Christmas carols and songs from the American Christmas repertoire arranged for banjo solo.

Tablature

The music in this book is for intermediate to advanced players, and assumes familiarity with how to read tablature. If you are not familiar with this system of notation, there are countless tutorials on the Internet. All the tunes are arranged in the standard banjo tuning of gDGBD.

Fingerings

I didn't mark any of the left-hand fingerings, although it's common to mark them in classical music notation; in general, the music is arranged in easy positions and you will not have to figure out many problems. A lot of these positions are common chords. For the right hand, it's another thing; in fact, it's the world as banjo fingerings are a topic of non-stop discussion. Over the years I've had many conversations with colleagues, especially about how to play fiddle tunes, and it's a great topic. For these tunes, I really think and play my fingerings like a classical guitarist, so I play the first string by alternating the index and middle fingers. I know I'm not playing by the usual banjo rules, but it's an option, maybe because I studied classical guitar.

Using the Recording

There are tempo suggestions on the page and a recording for each piece, yet some may sound better to your ears either faster or slower. Like all new music, I suggest learning these pieces at a slow tempo, and then increasing the speed.

Record Yourself

I encourage you to record yourself in both audio and video as a practice tool. We do not hear many details in the heat of the moment when playing. Looking or listening back provides evidence of how you are progressing with any piece. It may also alert you to some extraneous noises. The banjo provides lots of opportunities to make incidental noises, for example, your thumbpick hitting the head or metal picks striking the metal strings. In sparse music like the arrangements in this book, those noises may be more pronounced compared to a noisy bluegrass jam. Awareness is the first step needed to eliminate these issues. Often isolating just the right hand in practice at very slow tempos will help clear up some issues.

Interpretation

As you learn these pieces, the practice of interpretation becomes more important — i.e., making decisions beyond what the tablature indicates. In the age of the internet, we can stream many performances of any piece of music. Notice that each musician is playing the same notes but the performances are different; the differences are the result of interpretation. Sometimes in classical music, there are marks on the sheet music telling musicians how to interpret the piece, such as tempo, dynamics, articulation, emotions to exude, and even fingerings. These cues help us to play the music as the composer intended, and give heart and soul to the music. Aside from tempo, such cues are not included here. Your task is to listen to the pieces played as by several different artists and make your own artistic decisions about interpretation.

Acknowledgments

Thanks to all of my many banjo colleagues and students around the world, and an extra special thanks to the staff at Mel Bay Publications, Inc.: William, Sharon, Joanne, Josh, Connie, David, Julie, and Stephen.

Recorded by Lluís Gómez at Dotze Contes Studio
Mastering by Jordi "Kako" Vericat at JK Music
Lluís Gómez plays and endorses Prucha banjos.

Contents

A Virgin Unspotted

Allegro ♩ = 140

Early American Carol
Arr. Lluis Gómez

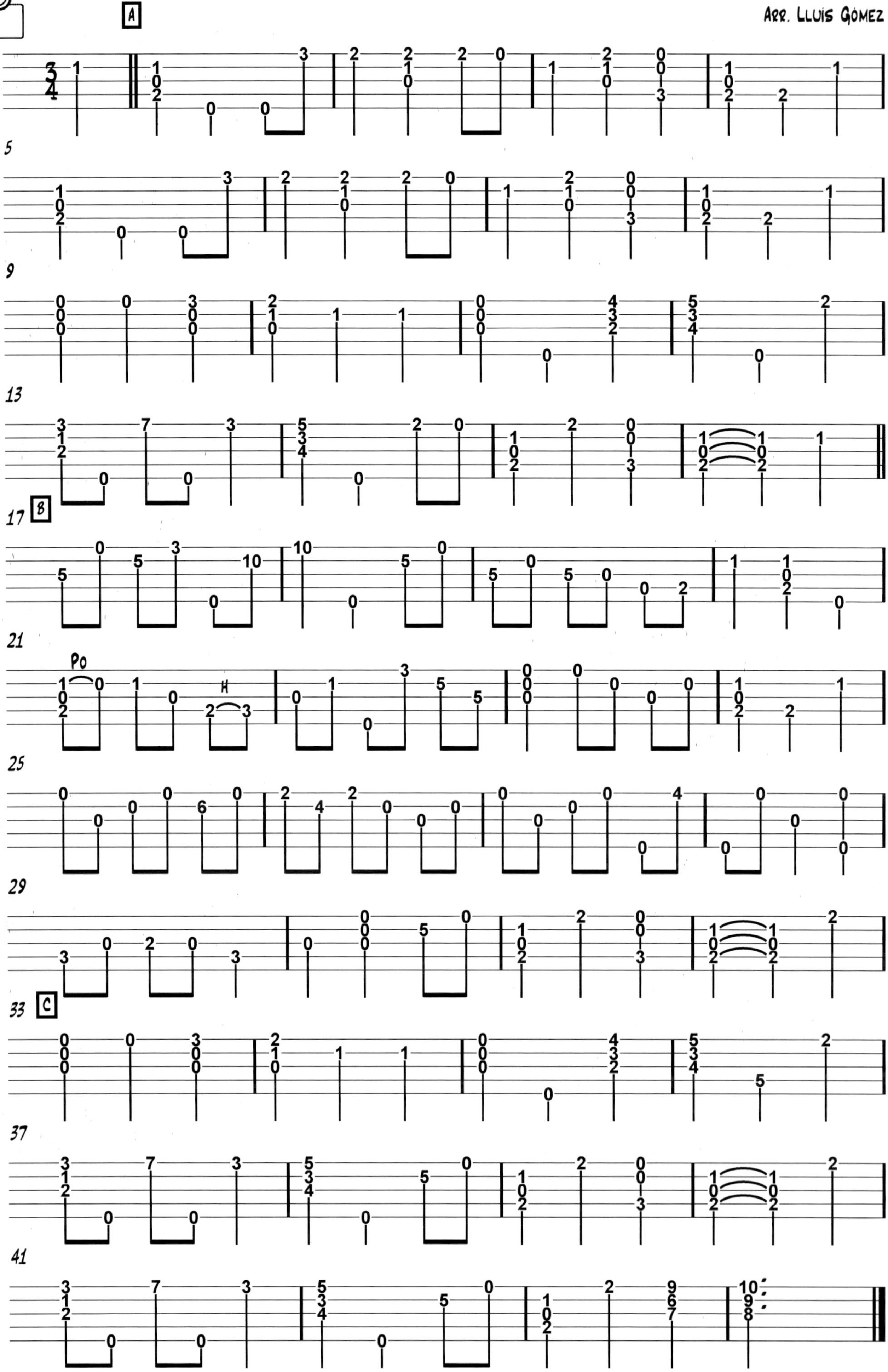

Away in a Manger

2

Gently ♩ = 72

James R. Murray
Arr. Lluis Gómez

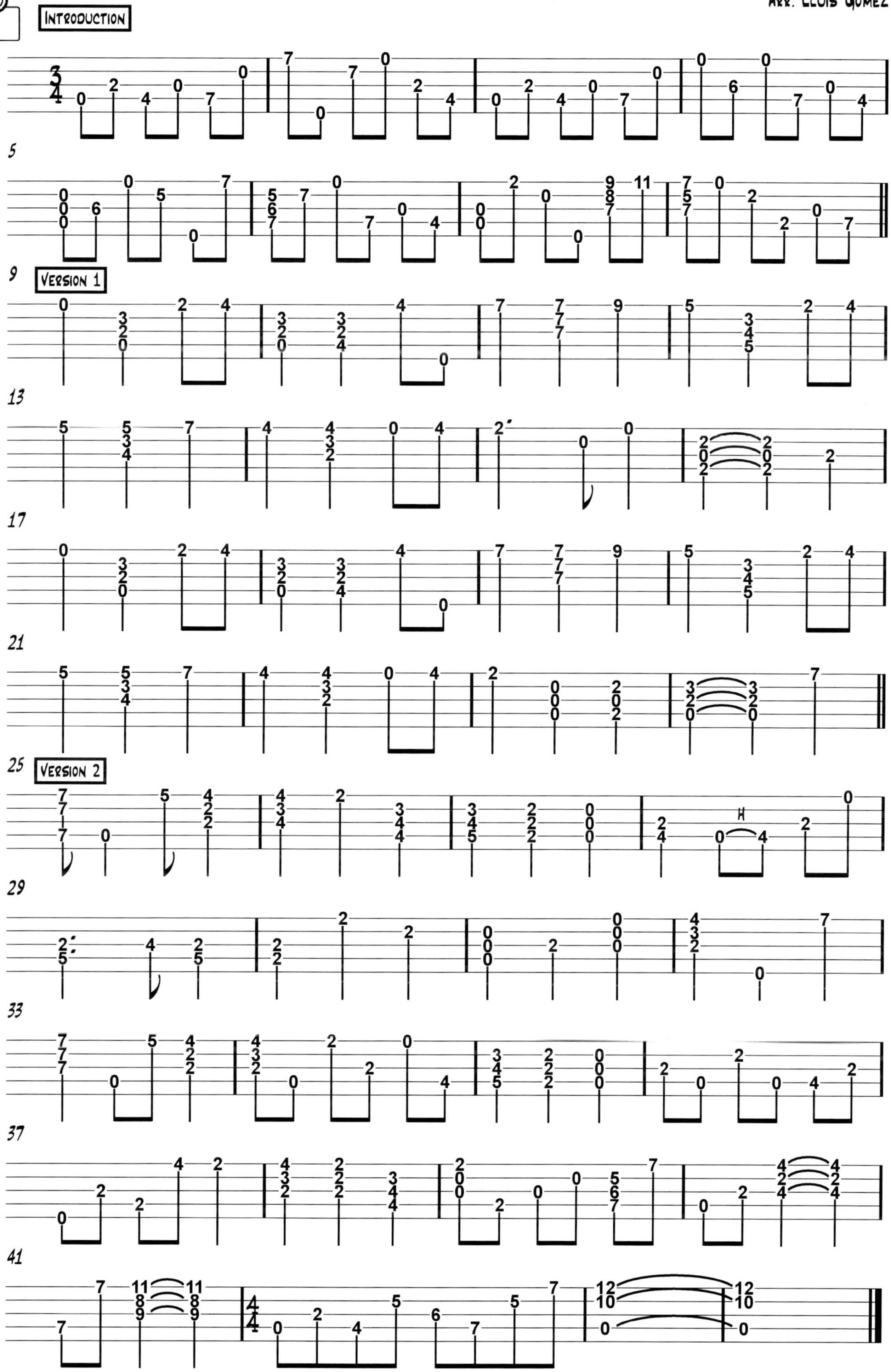

Beautiful Star

3

Relaxed Feeling ♩. = 72

D. B. Towner
Arr. Lluis Gomez

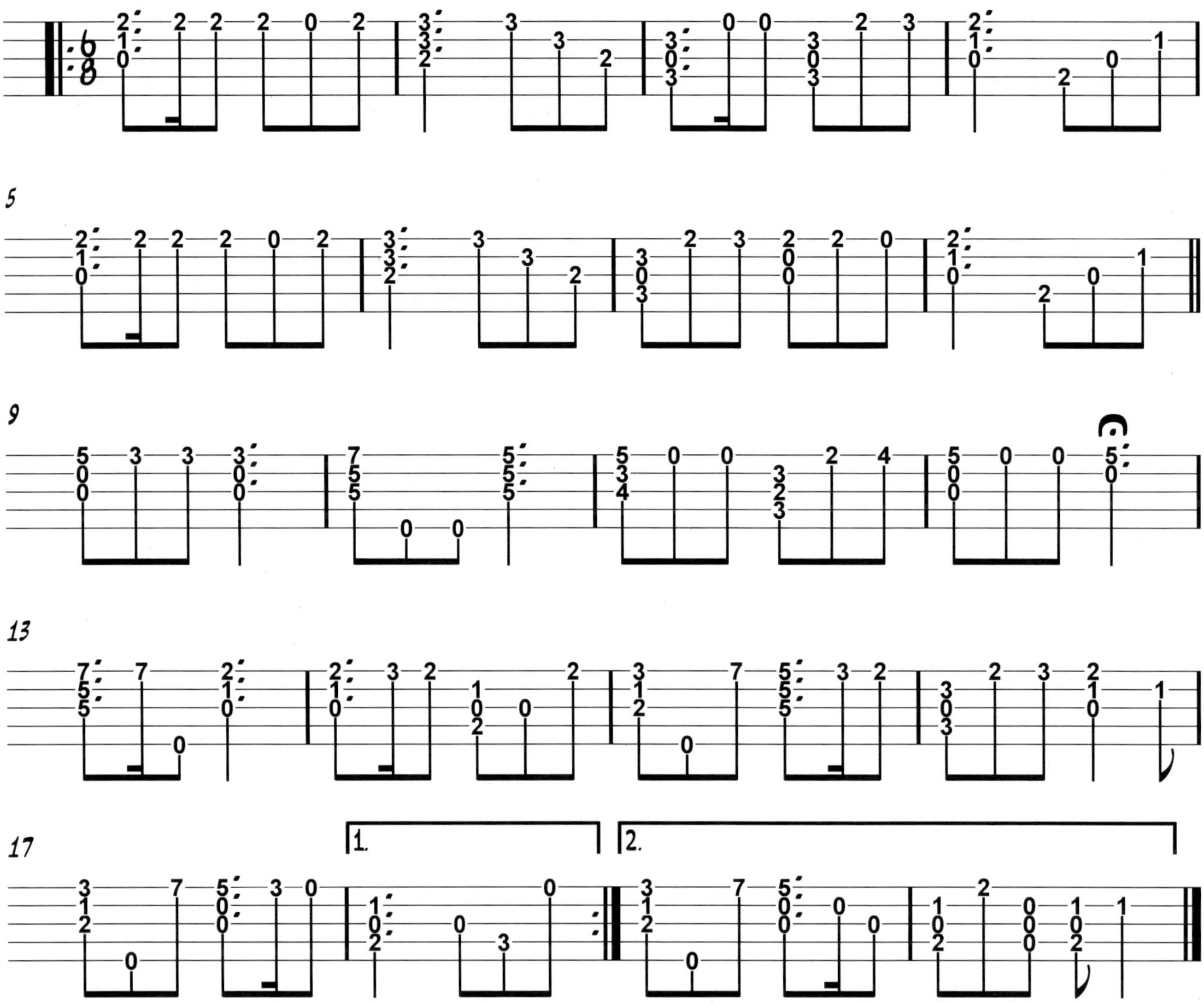

This page has been left blank to avoid an awkward page turn.

EXALTATION

Early American Shaped-Note Hymn
Arr. Lluis Gomez

Andante ♩ = 88

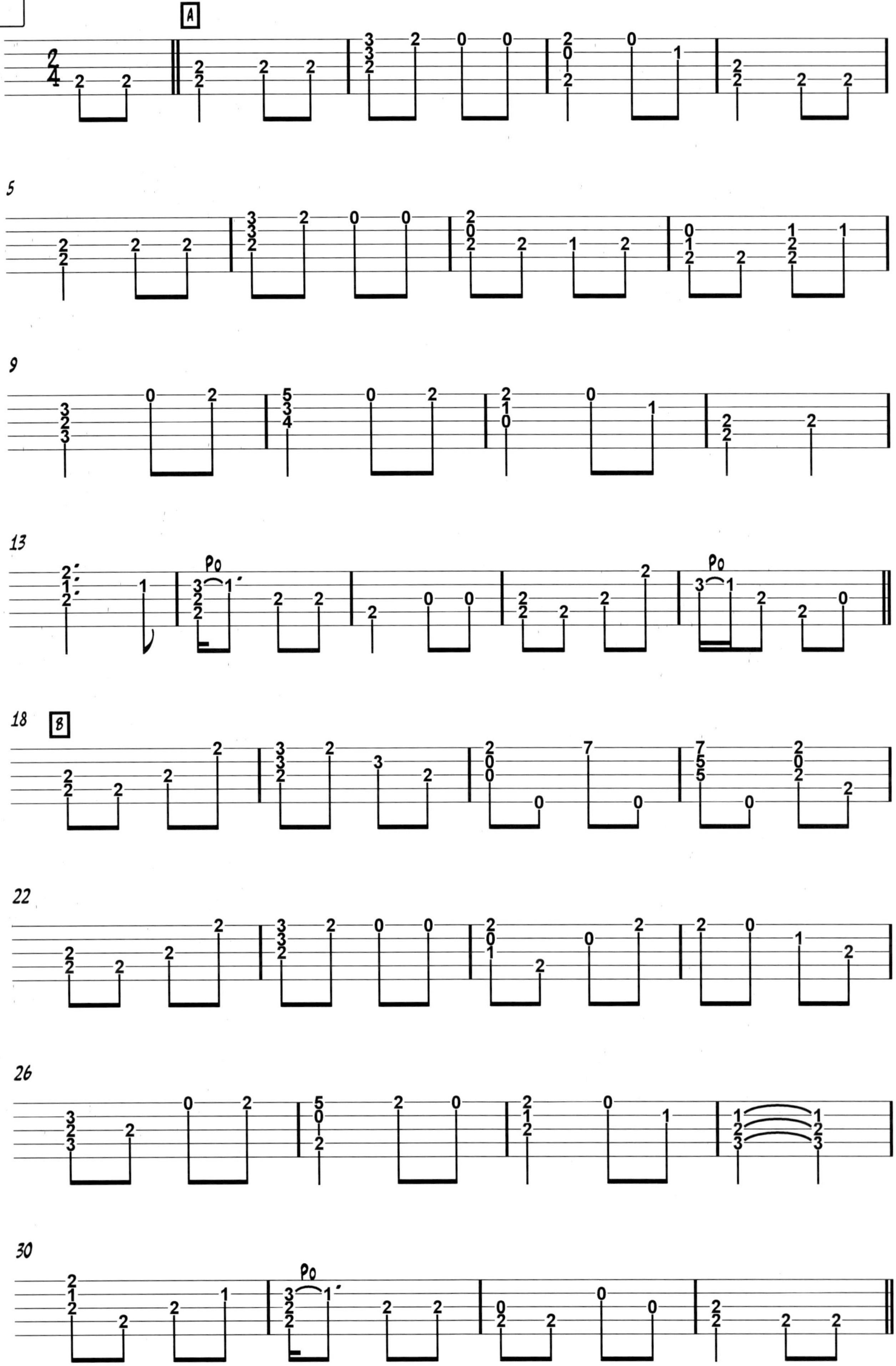

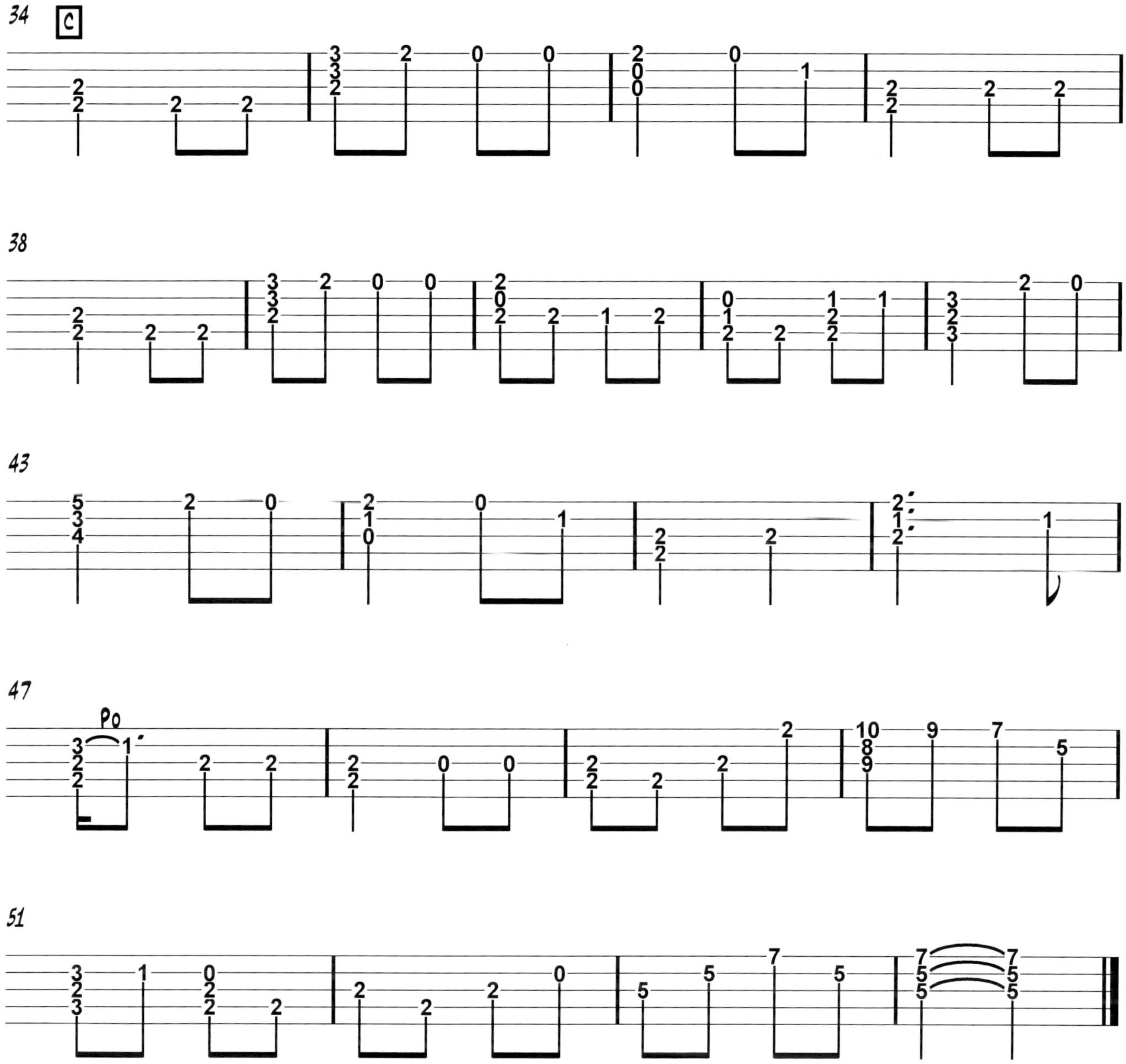
34
C
38
43
47
Po
51

5

Go Tell It on the Mountain

American Spiritual
Arr. Lluis Gomez

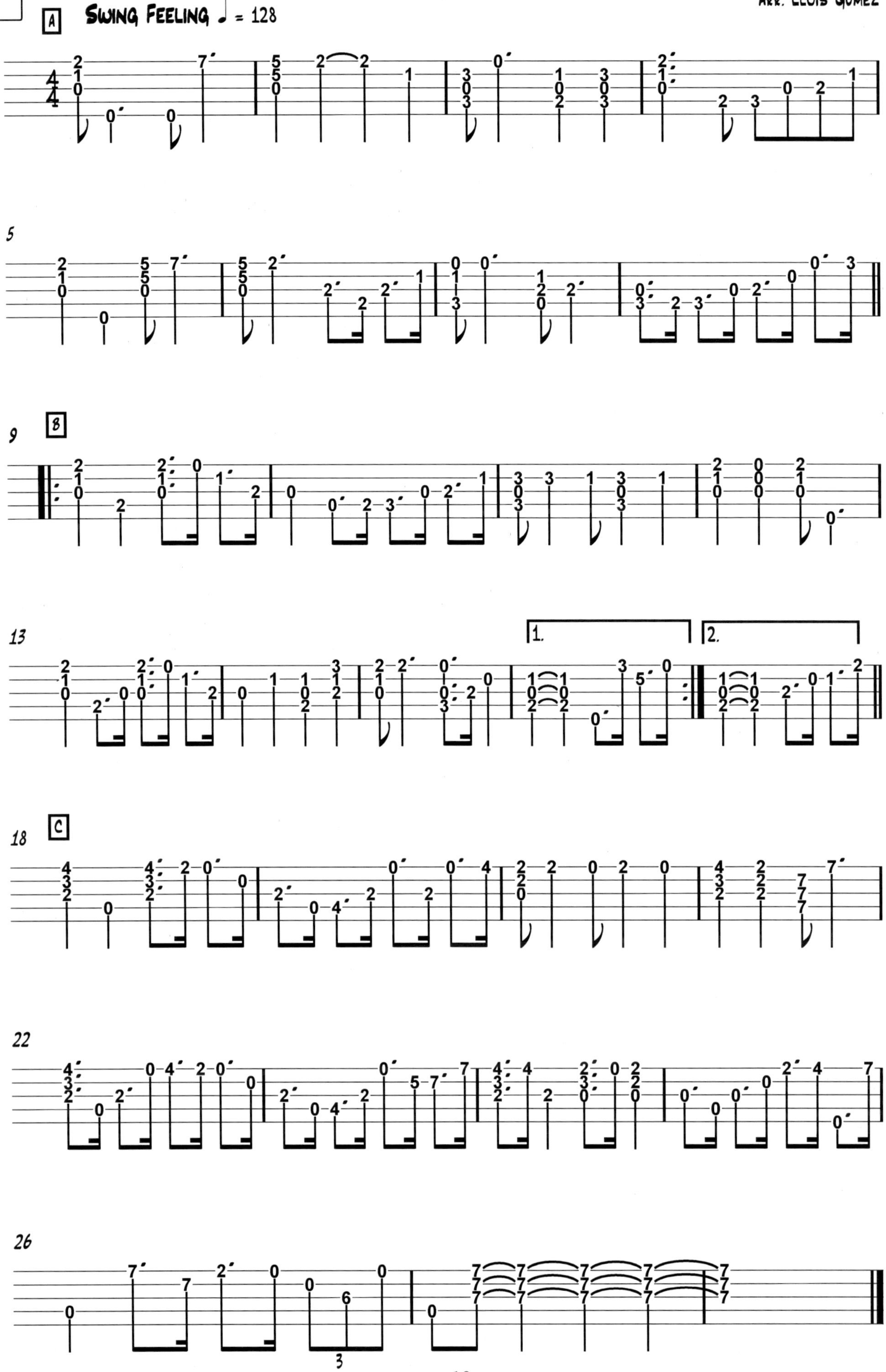

6

Hush My Babe, Lie Still and Slumber

Southern Harmony, 1835
Arr. Lluis Gómez

Andante ♩ = 80

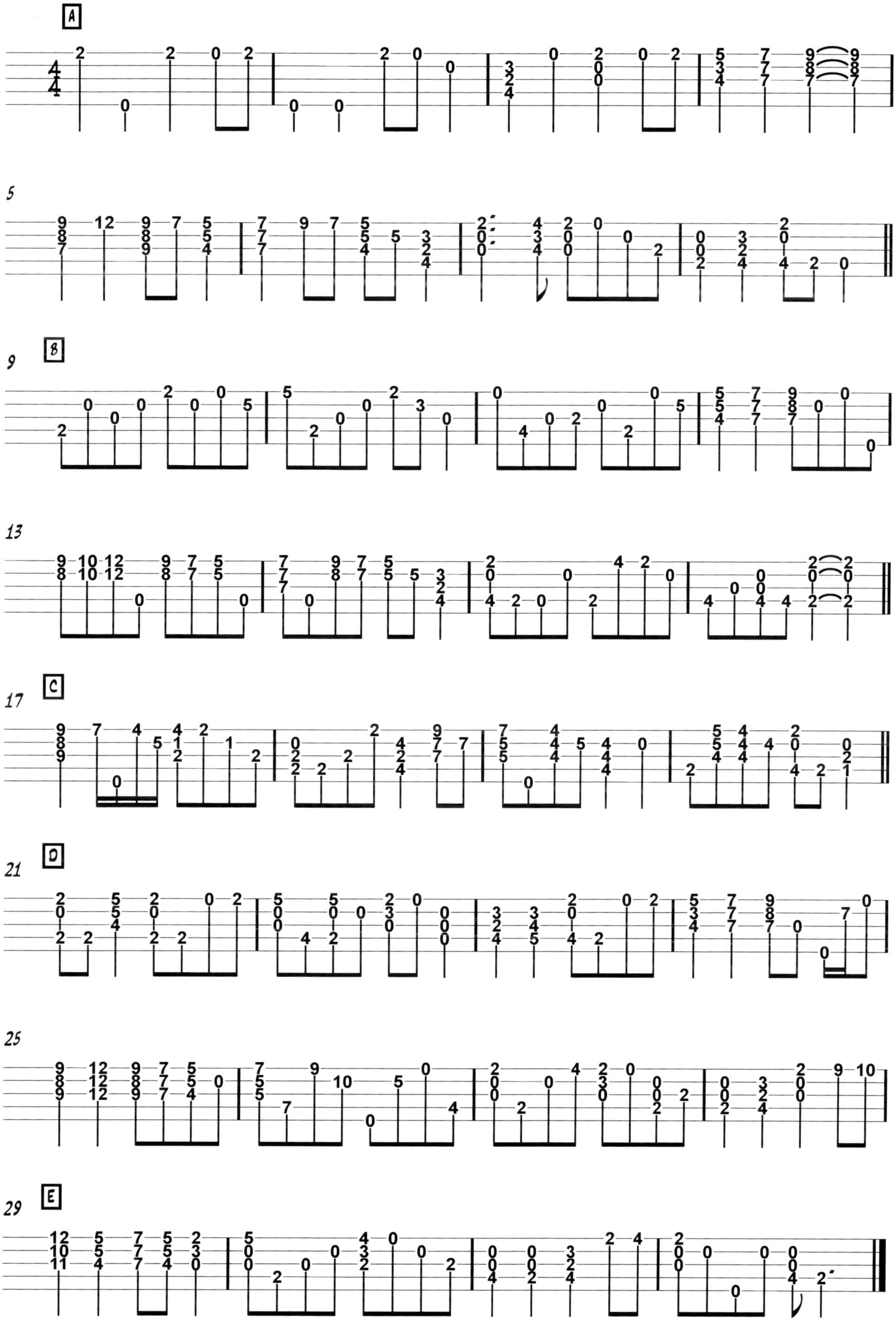

Great Creator

Slowly 𝅗𝅥 = 90

Early American Hymn
Arr. Lluis Gómez

7

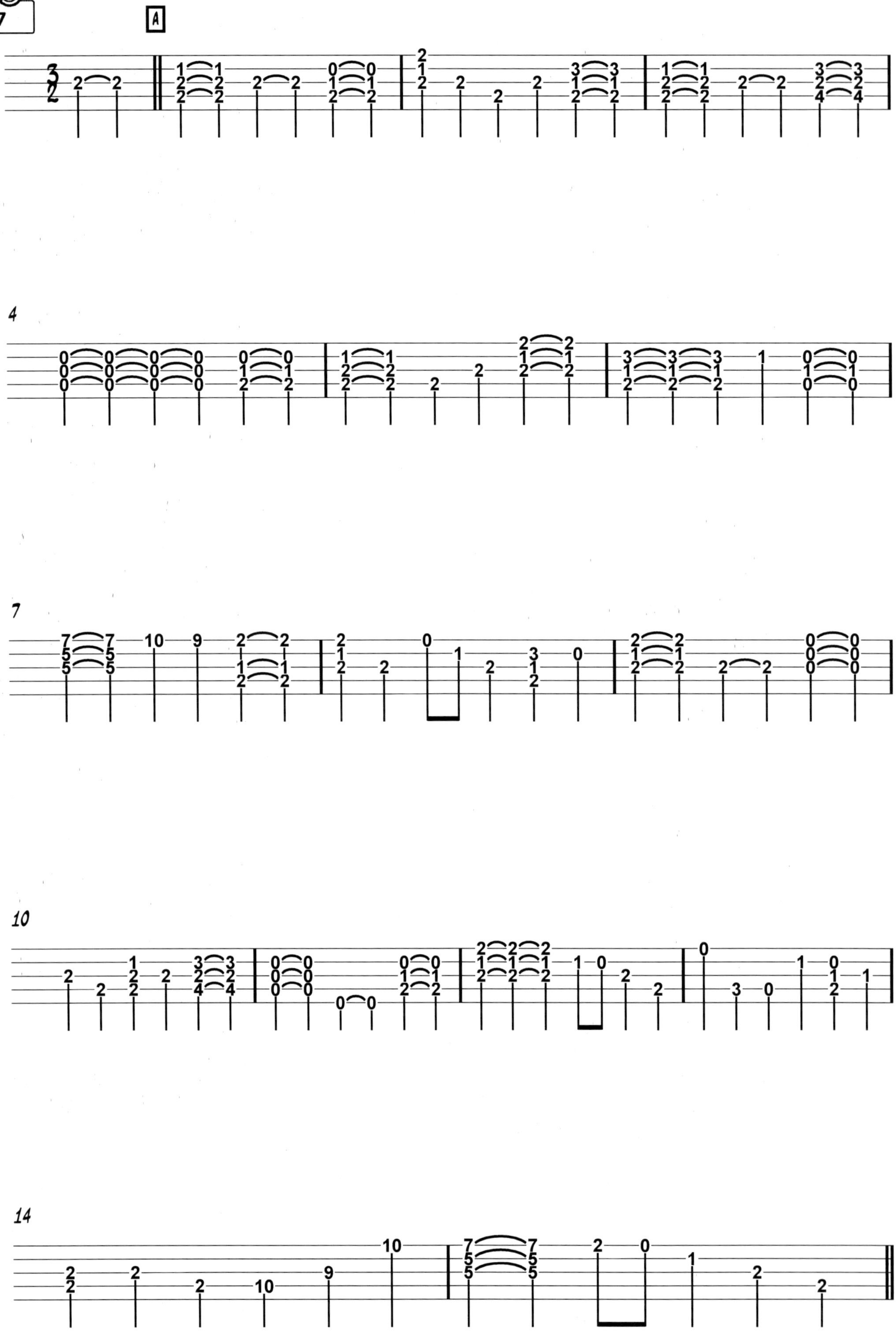

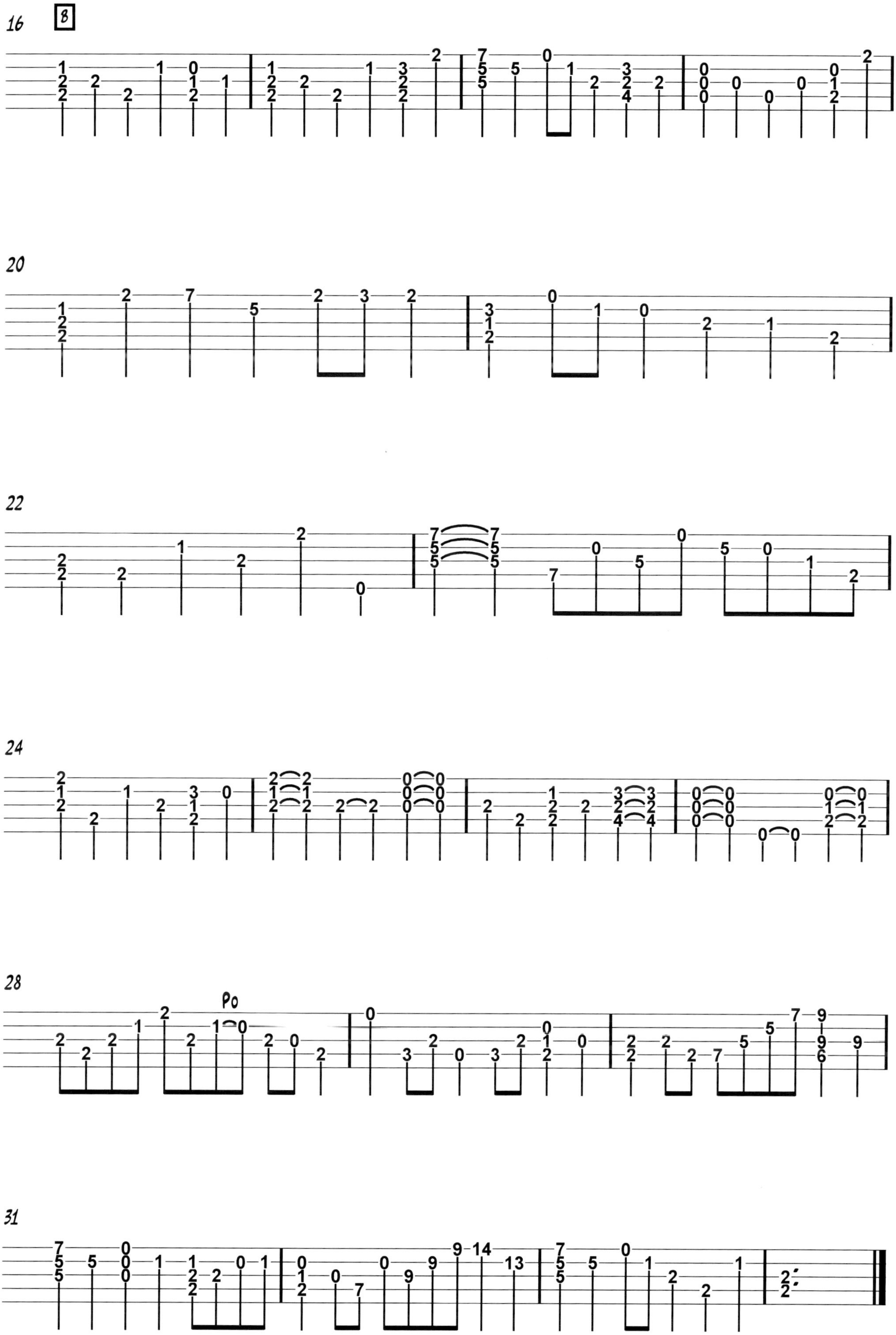
16
B
20
22
24
28
Po
31

8

It Came Upon a Midnight Clear

Lyrically ♩ = 100

Richard Storrs Willis
Arr. Lluis Gómez

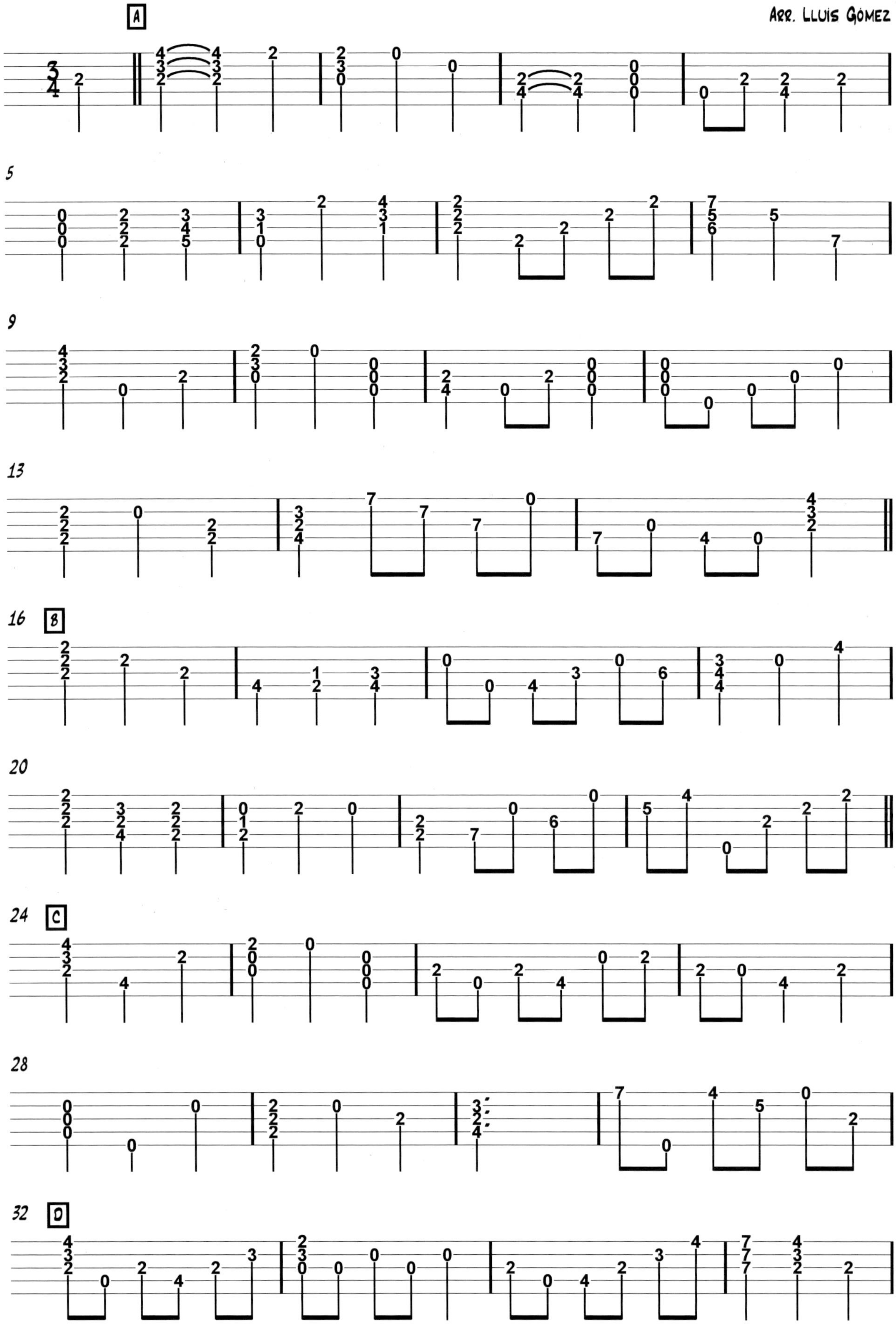

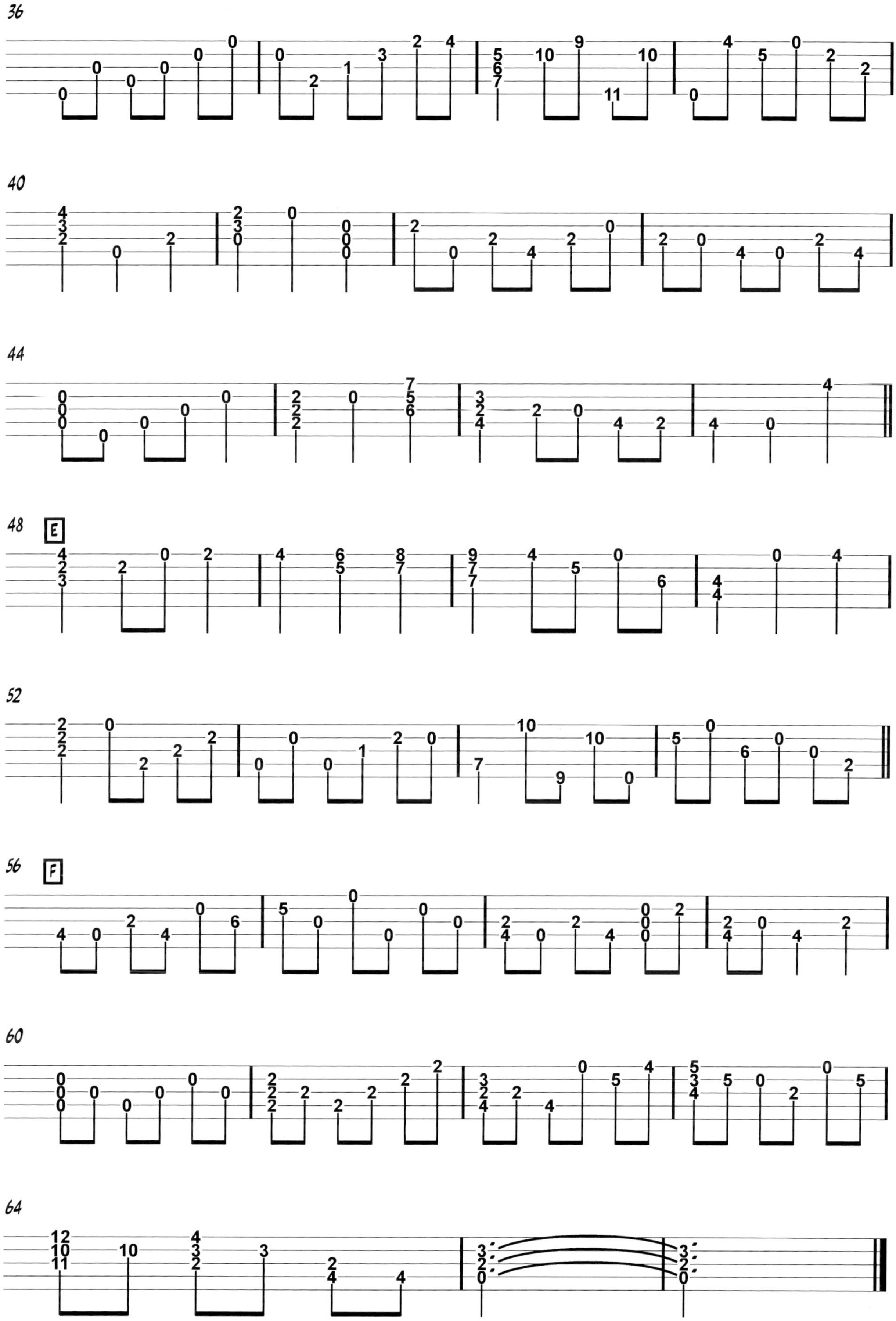
36
40
44
48
E
52
56
F
60
64

9

Lancaster

Rhythmically ♩. = 60

Early American Carol
Arr. Lluis Gómez

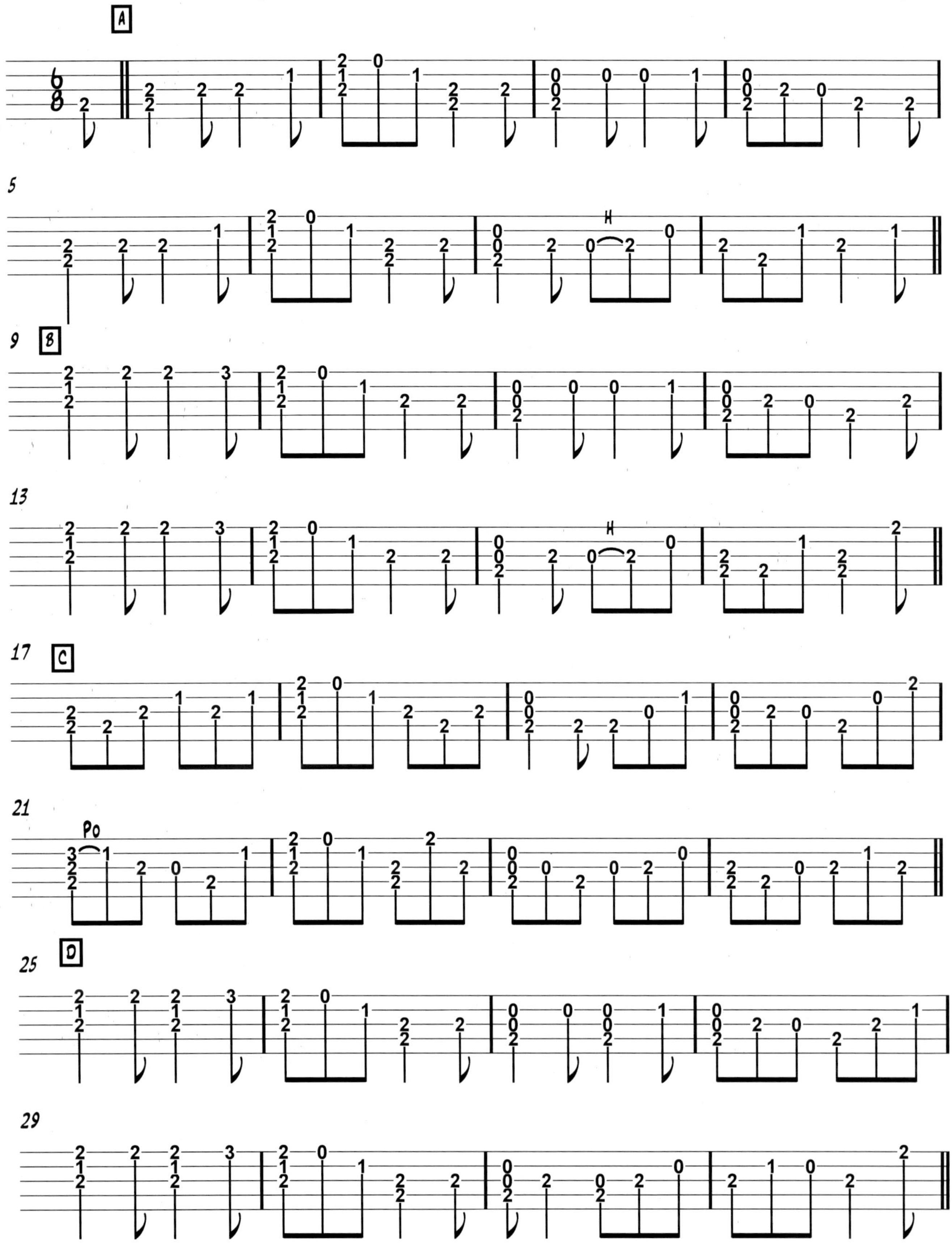

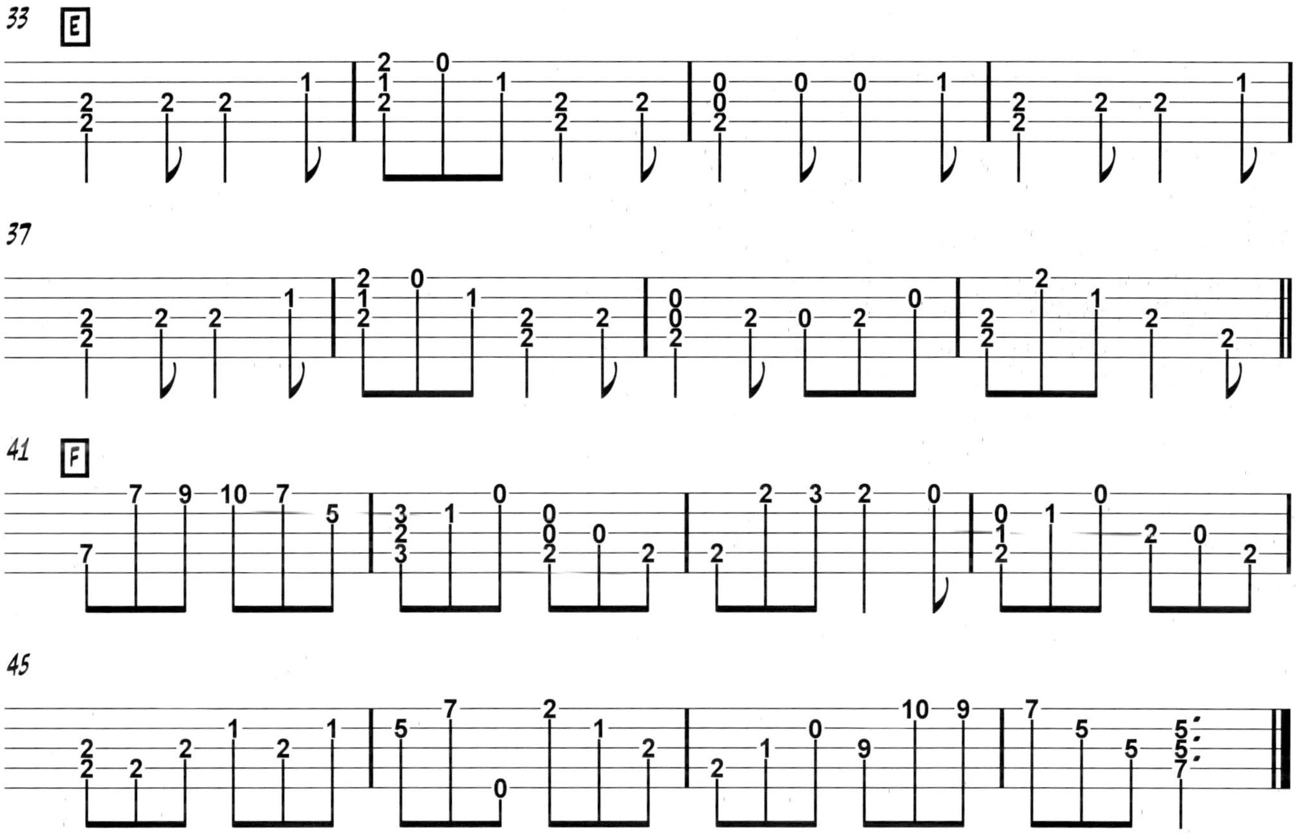
E
F

10

Mary Had a Baby/ What Yo' Gonna Call Your Pretty Little Boy?

Medley

American Spirituals
Arr. Lluís Gómez

♩ = 90

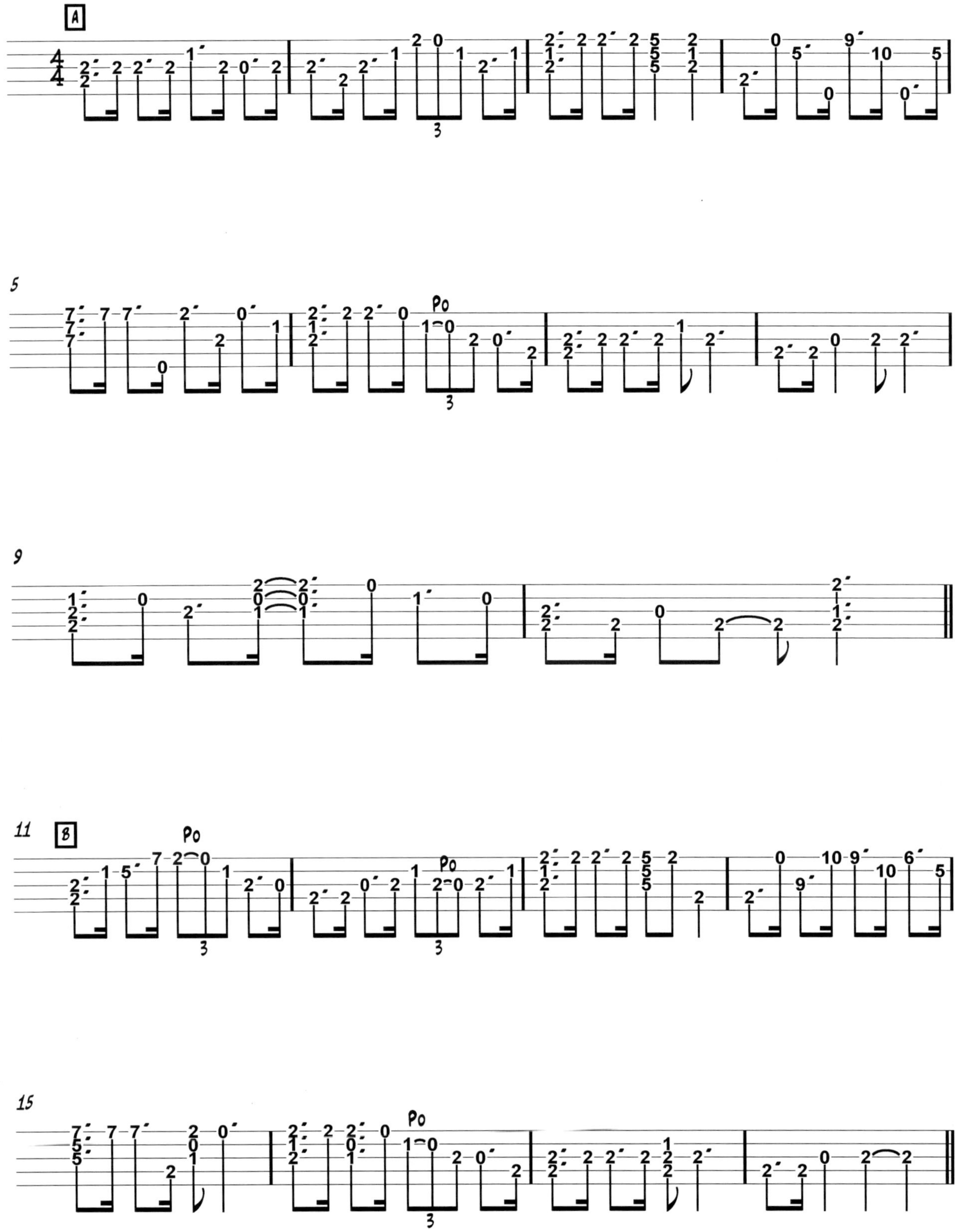

What Yo' Gonna Call Your Pretty Little Boy?

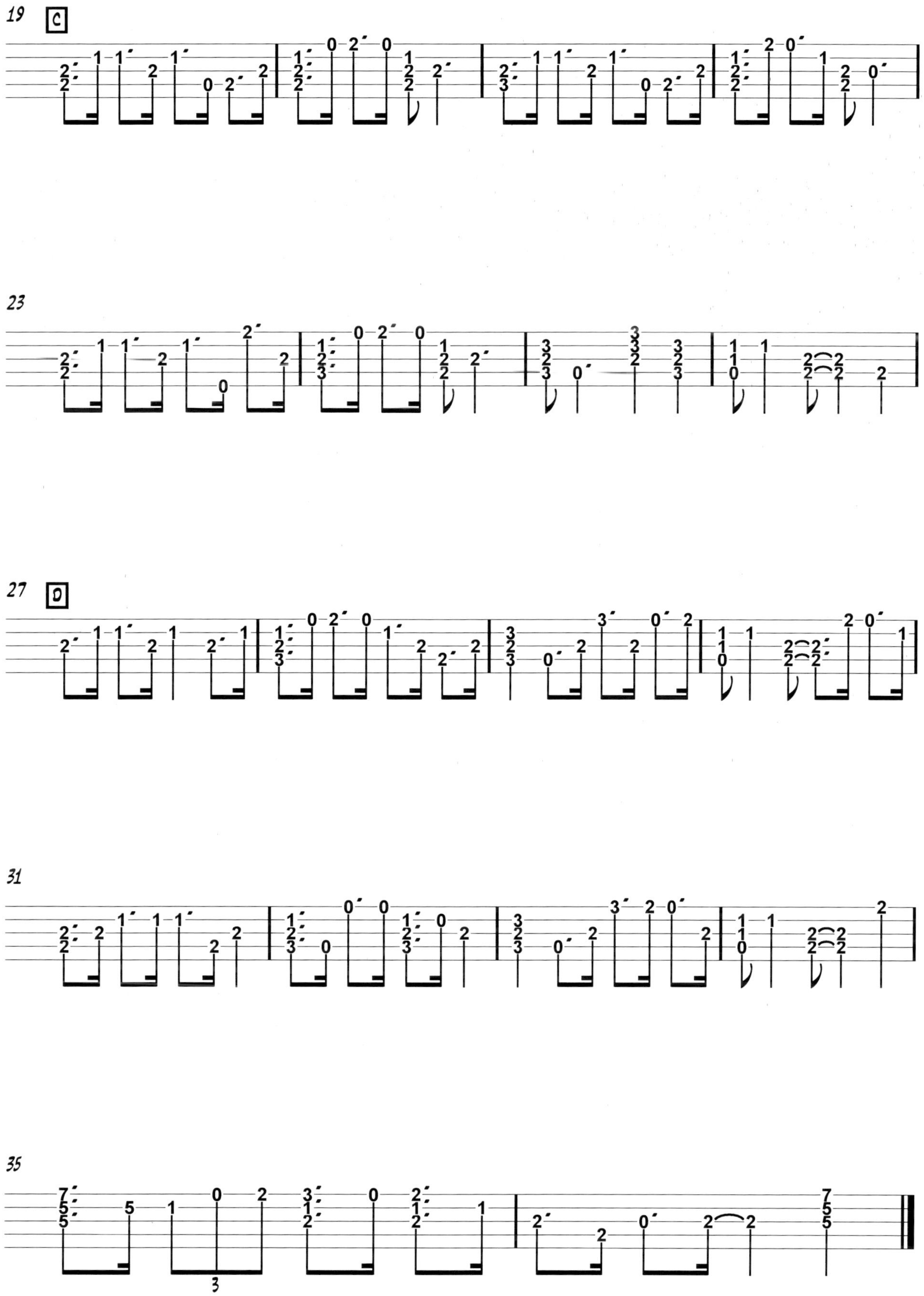

11

Andante ♩ = 72

O Little Town of Bethlehem
(St. Louis)

Lewis H. Redner
Arr. Lluis Gómez

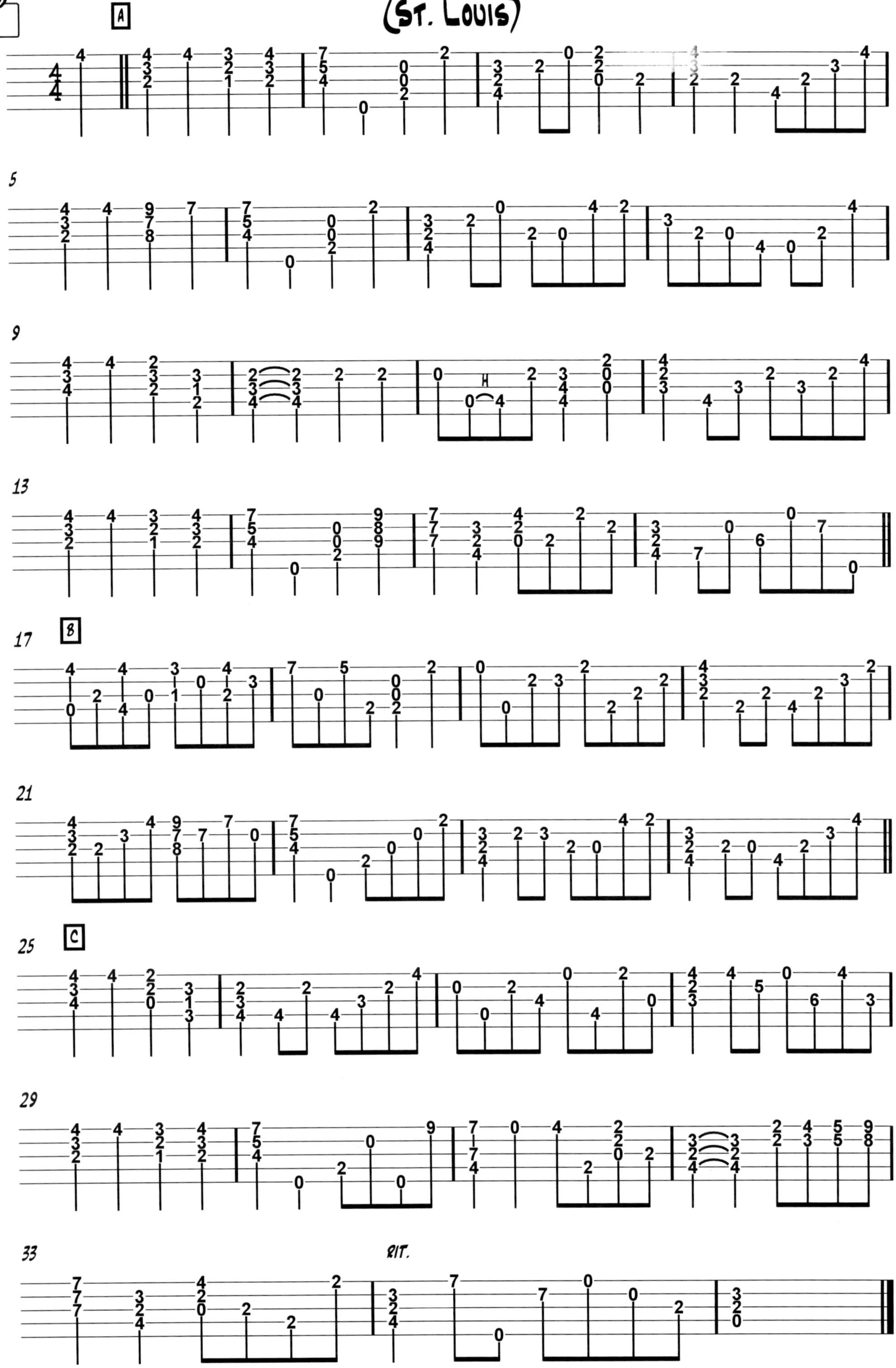

12

Rise Up, Shepherd and Follow

American Spiritual
Arr. Lluis Gomez

Easy Swing Feeling ♩ = 120

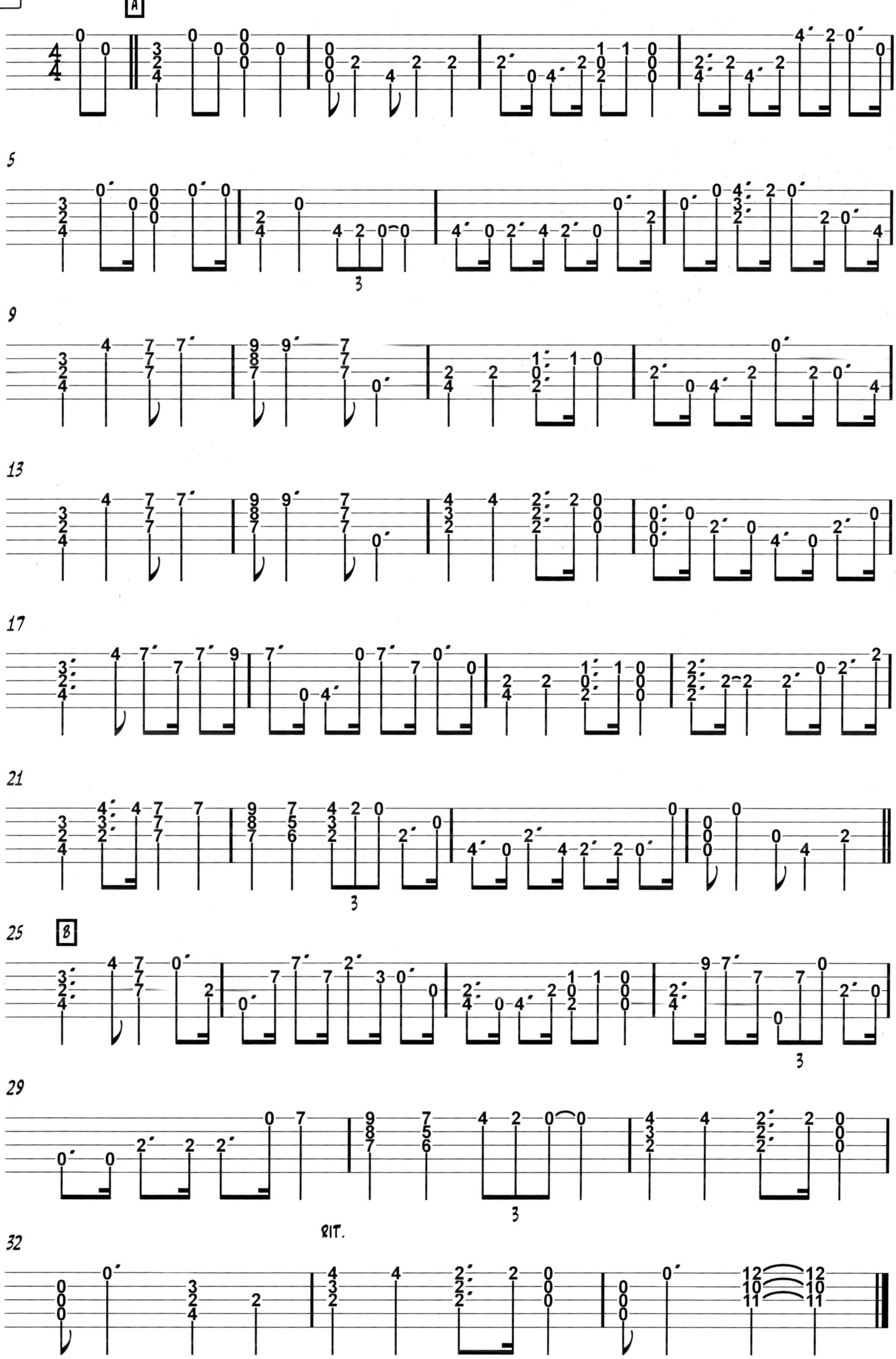

13

Star in the East

Moderato ♩ = 100

Early American Carol
Arr. Lluís Gómez

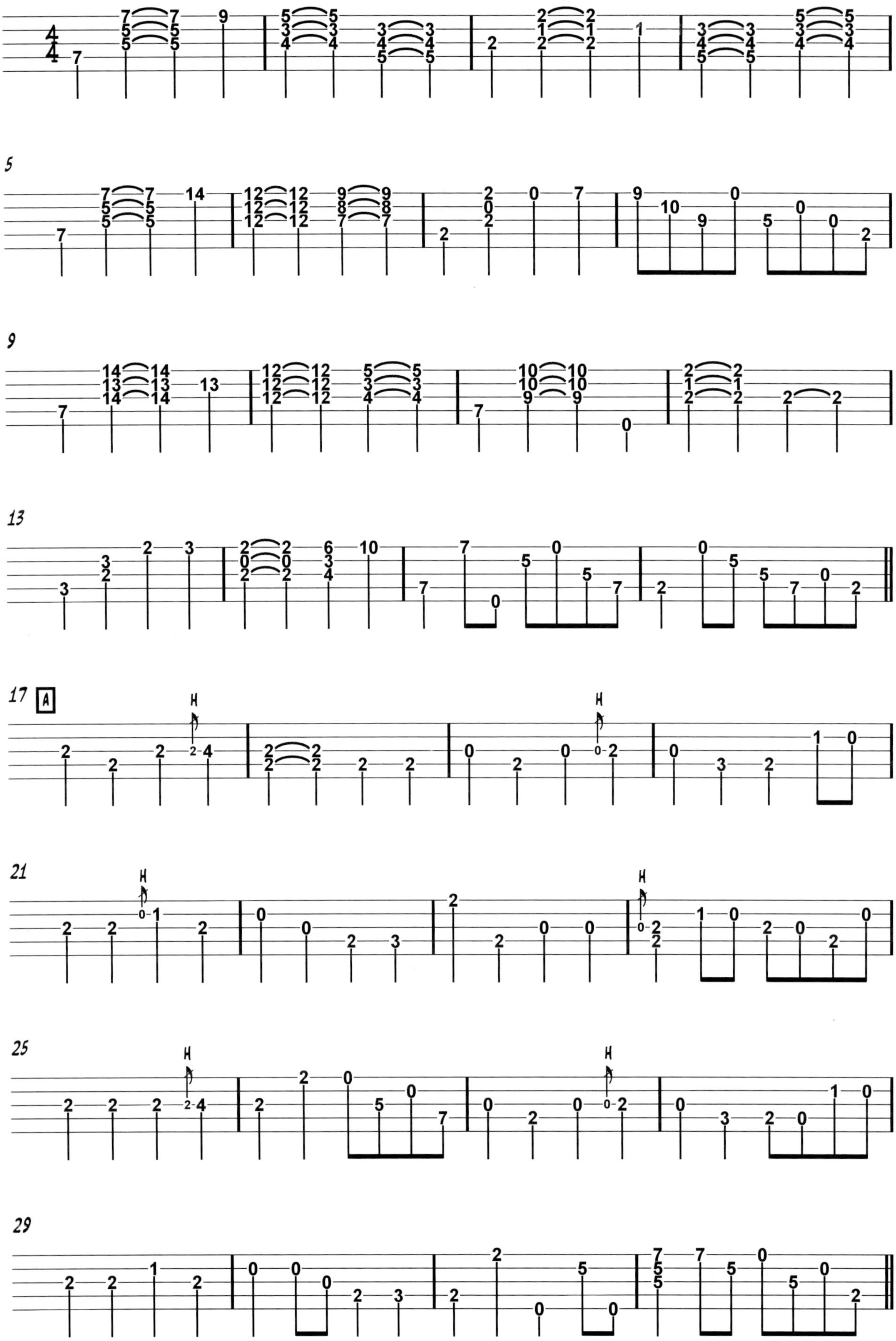

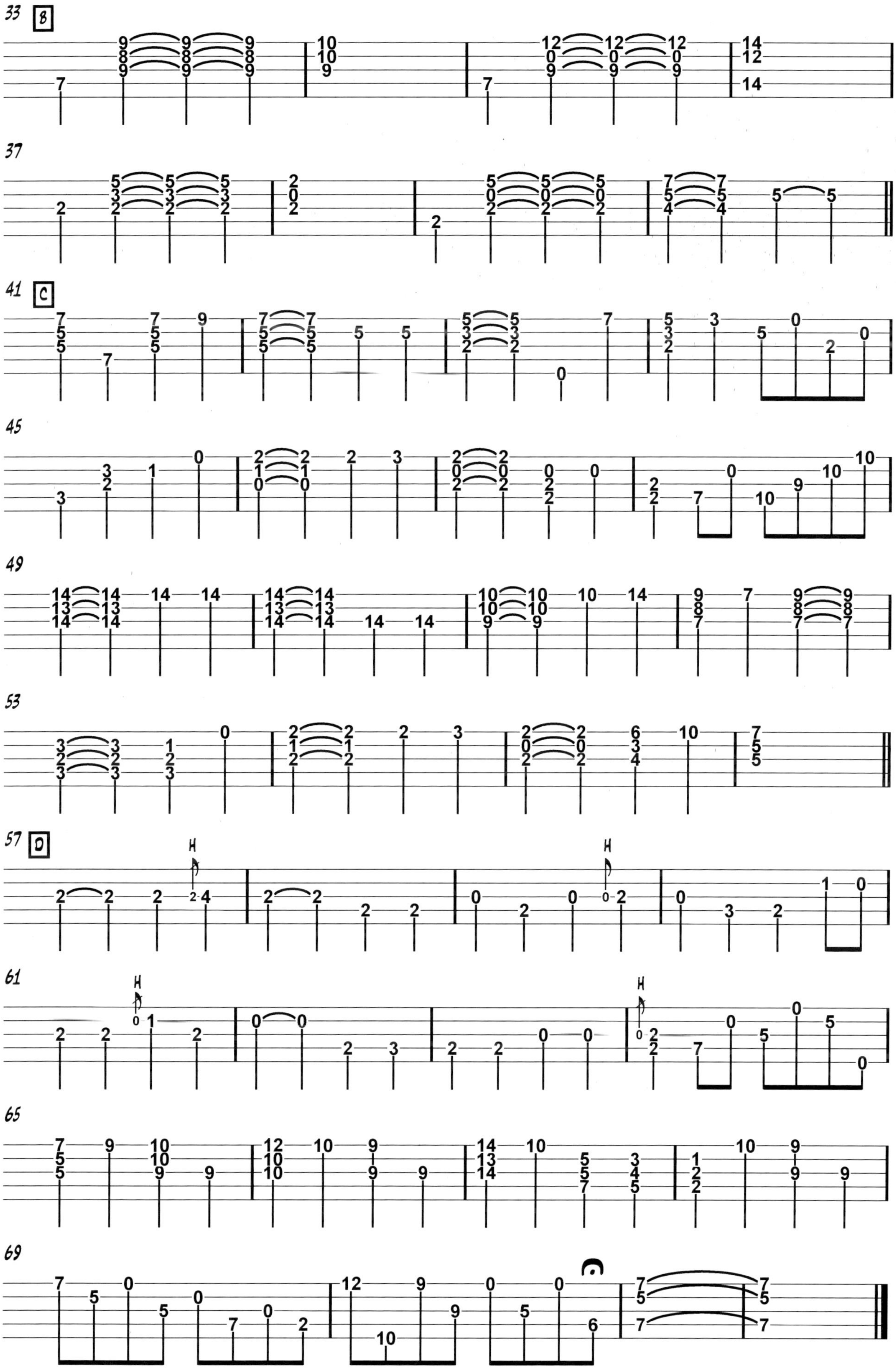

14

FLOWING TEMPO ♩. = 65

THE BABE OF BETHLEHEM

EARLY AMERICAN CAROL
ARR. LLUIS GÓMEZ

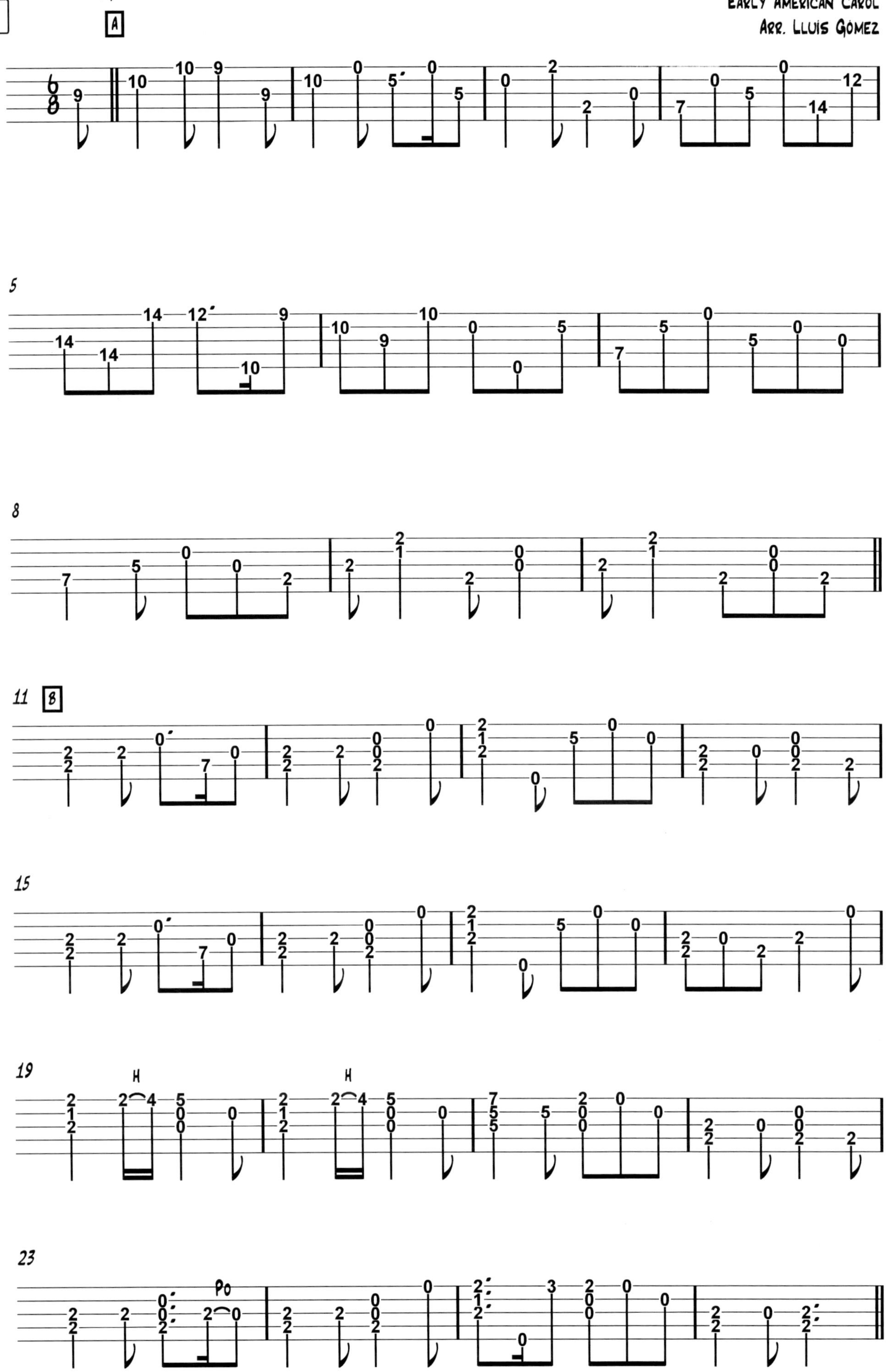

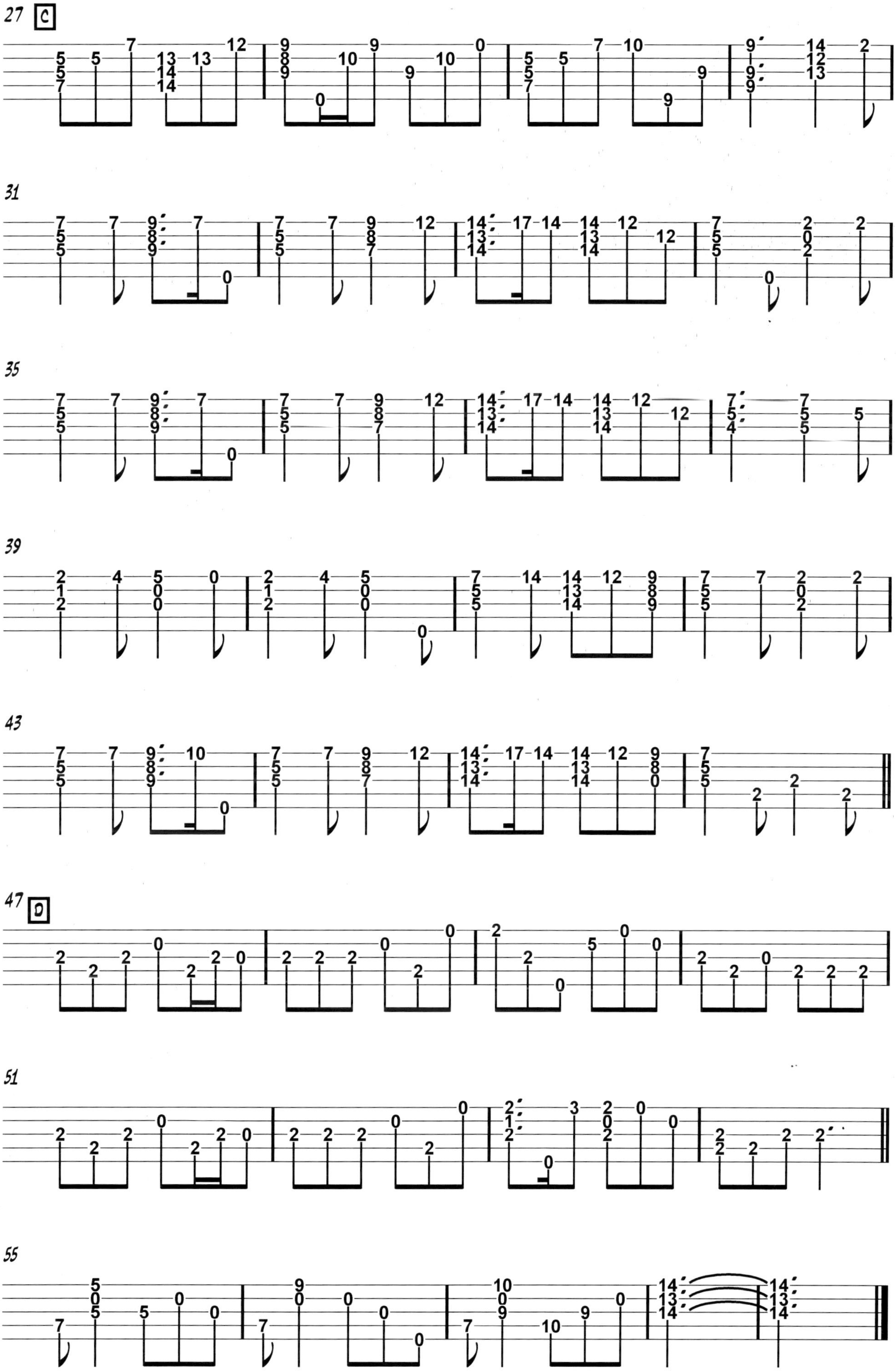
27 C
31
35
39
43
47 D
51
55

15

The Cherry Tree Carol

Slowly ♩ = 70

Early American Carol
Arr. Lluis Gómez

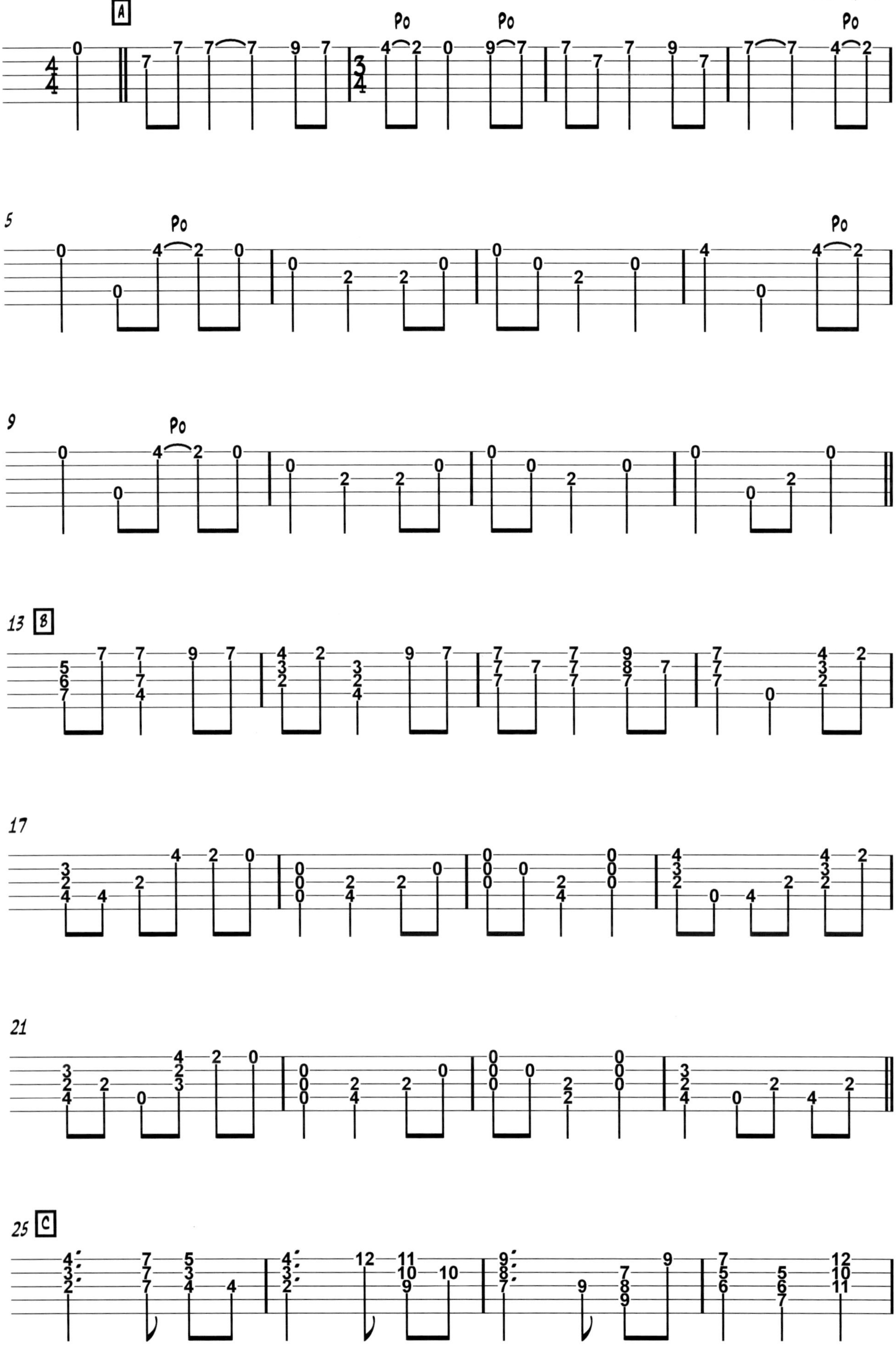

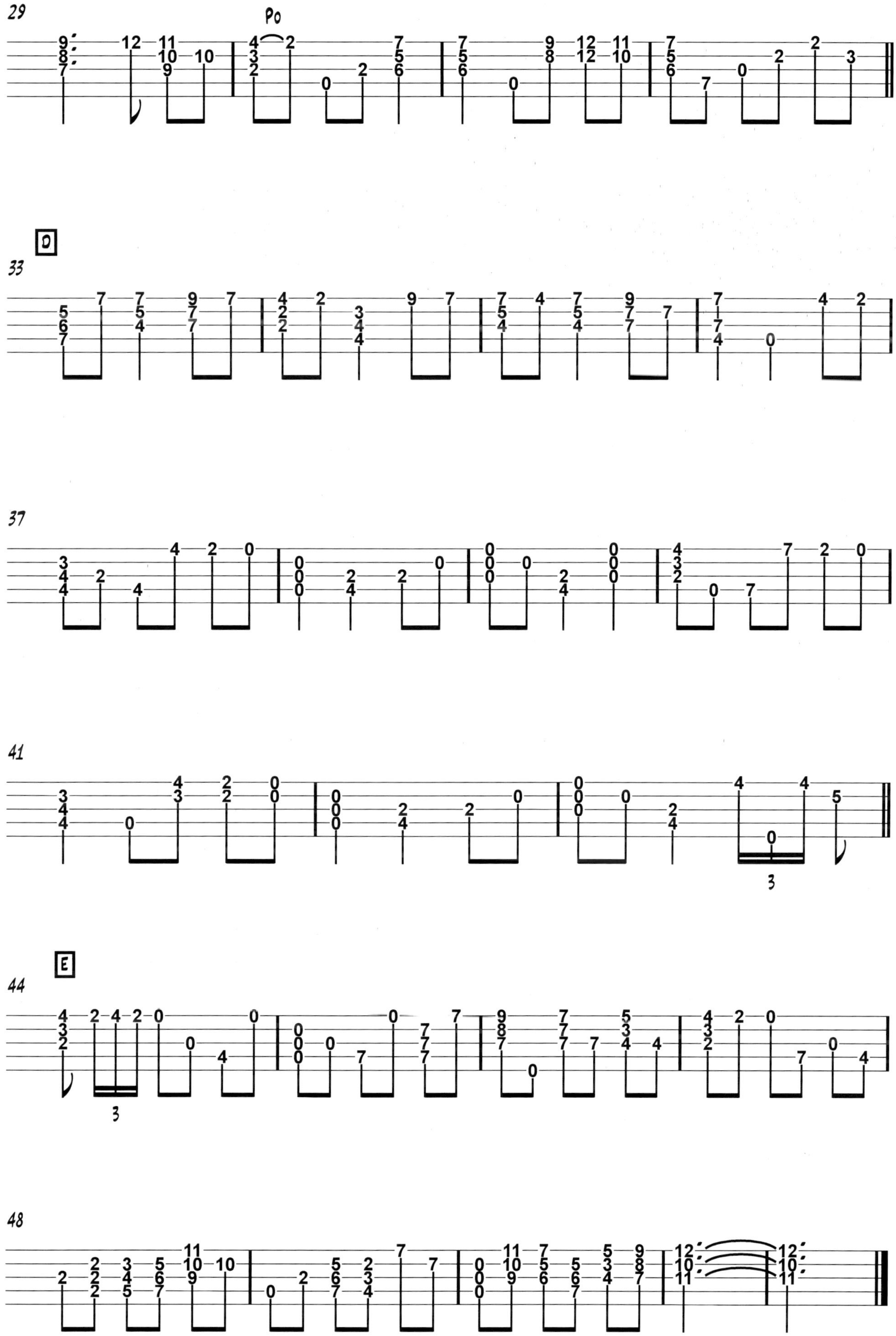
Po
D
E

16

The Shepherds' Star

Moderately ♩ = 100

Early American Carol
Arr. Lluís Gómez

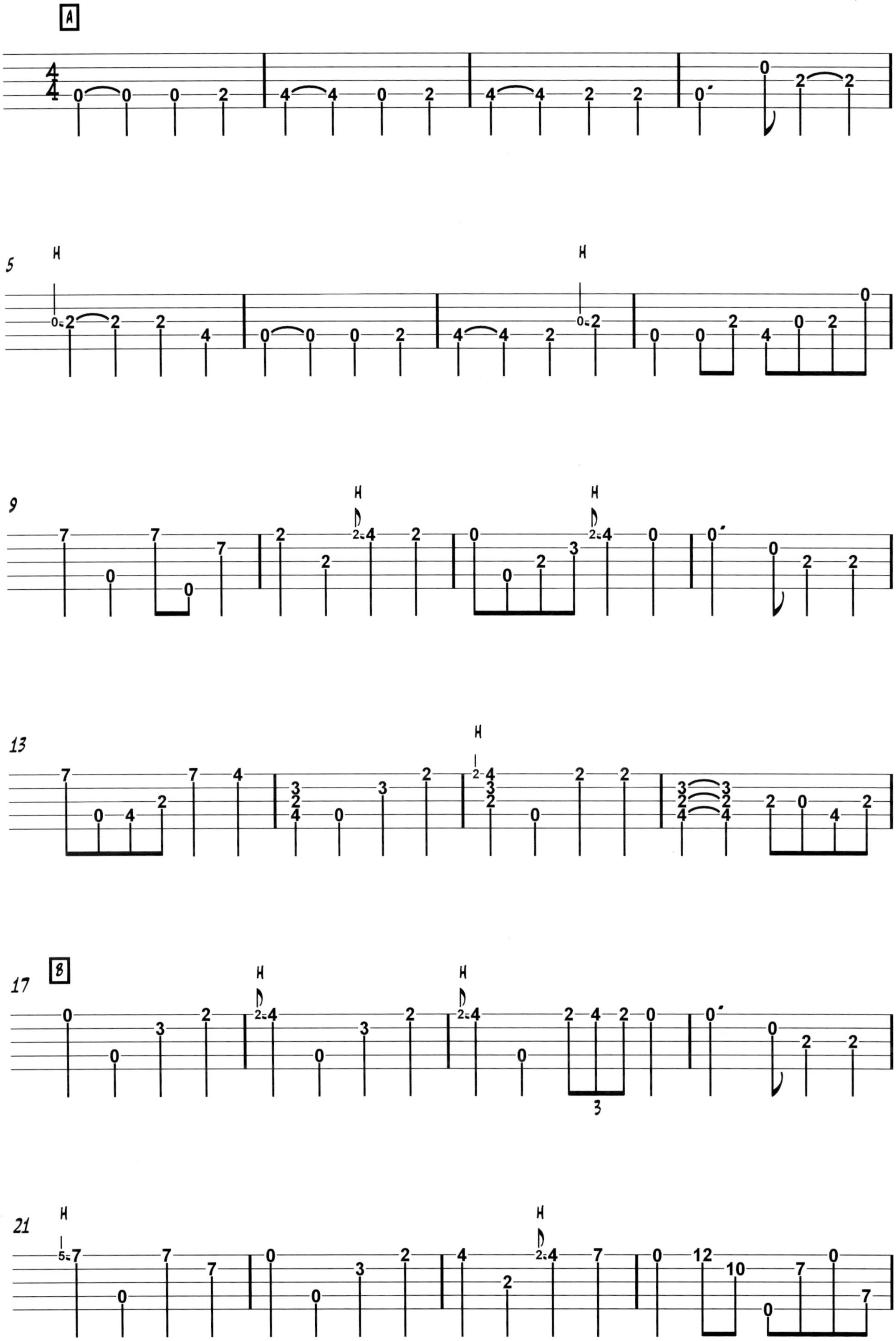

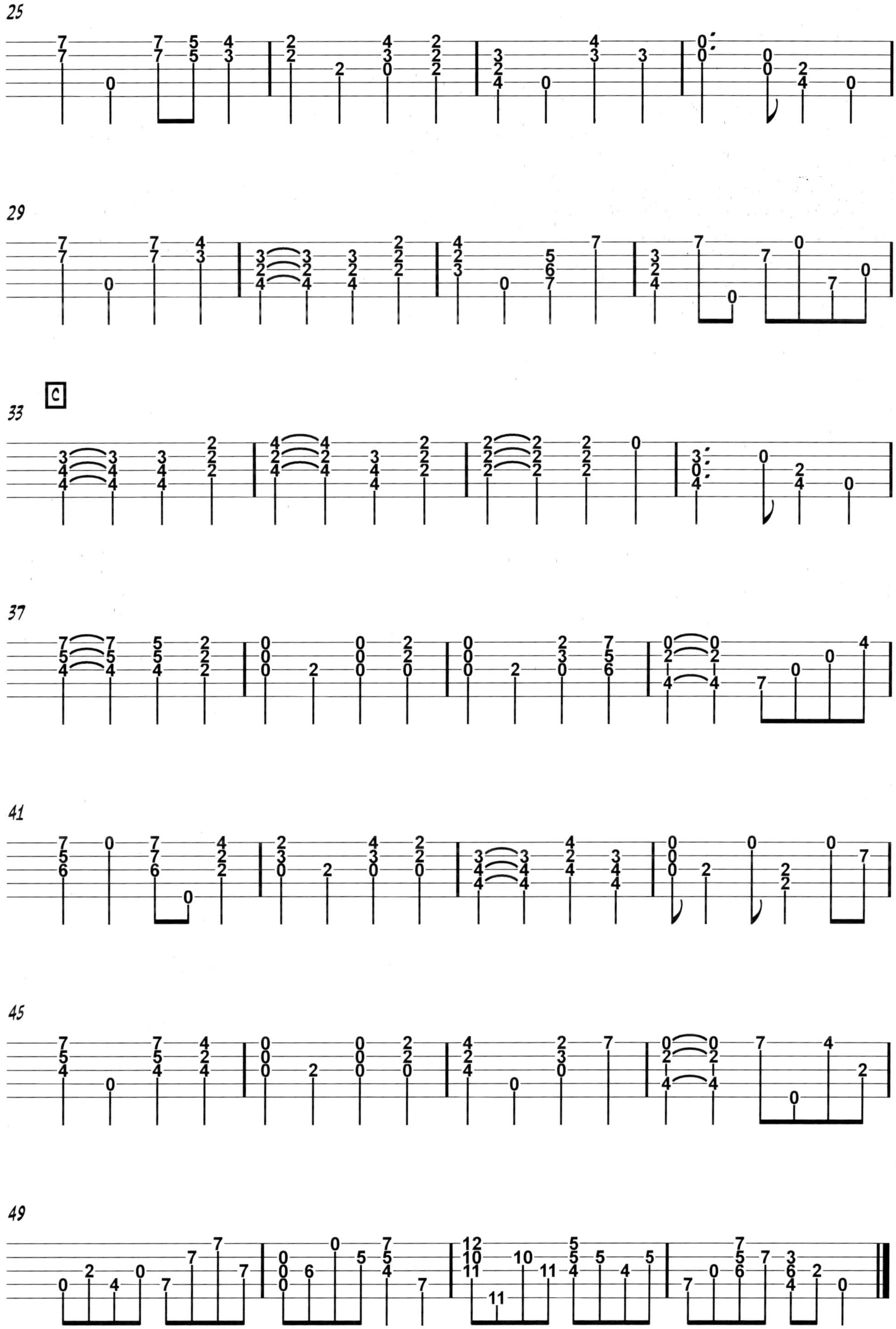

17

Moderato ♩ = 112

The Huron Carol

Arr. Lluís Gómez

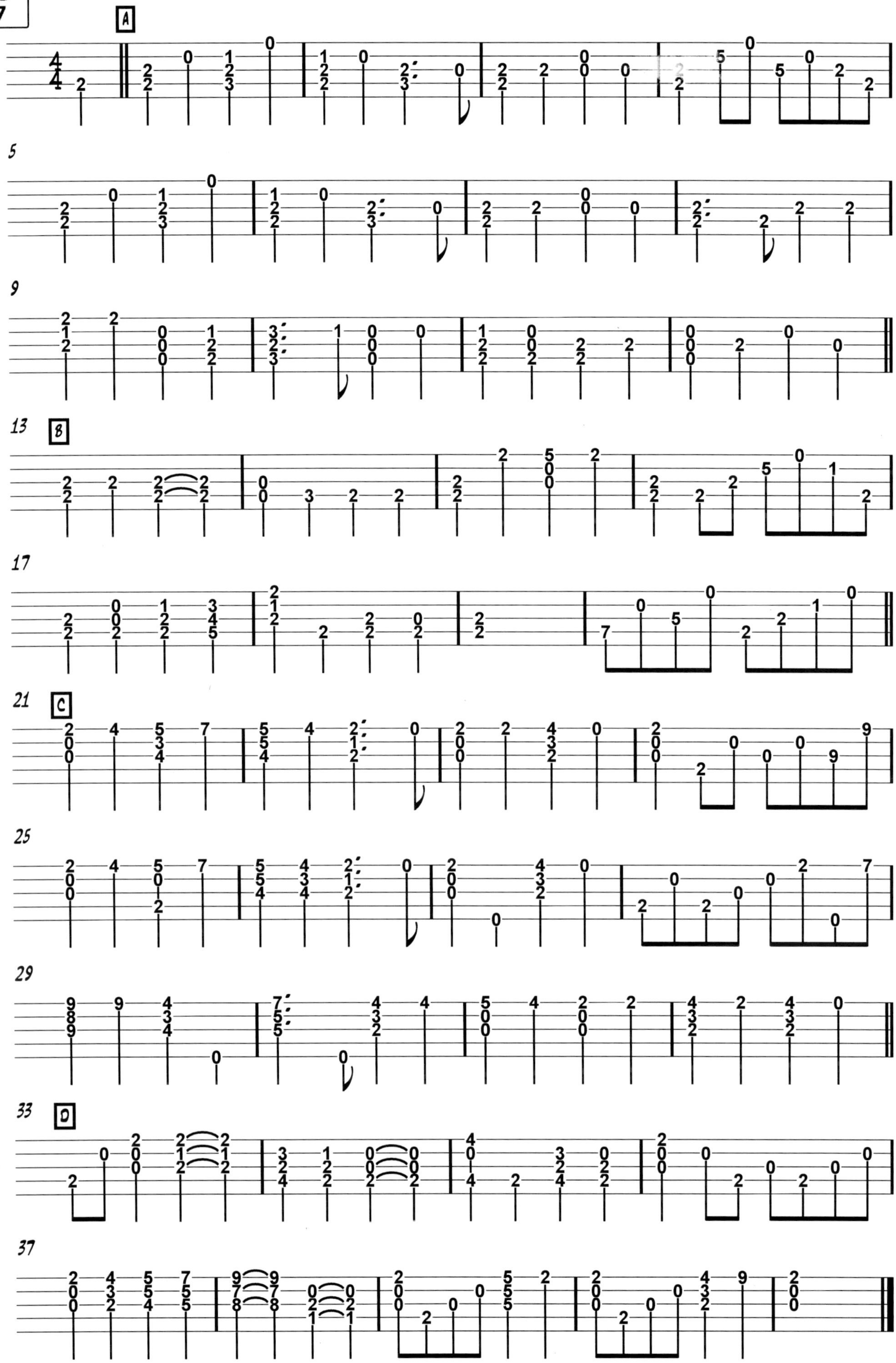

About the Author

Lluís Gómez

Photo Courtesy of Laura Ruiz

At an early age and largely encouraged by the musical atmosphere in his family, Lluís Gómez began teaching himself the acoustic guitar and the electric bass. He studied two years of flute and went on to study classical guitar at the age of 18 with Pere Payes at the Music School of Premià de Mar (Catalonia, Spain), and subsequently took up the electric guitar with Josep Traver. He also studied modern harmony with Ramón Montoliu at the Badalona Municipal School of Music. At the age of 30 he began learning the fiddle, at first self-taught and then formally with Raúl Munizaga.

The discovery of bluegrass through the *Banjo Paris Session* album was a watershed in his career. He was so taken by this style that he immediately picked up the five-string banjo and took lessons from Sedo Garcia and Ricky Araiza in Barcelona. He then travelled to France, Ireland, the UK and the US to take lessons from Jean Marie Redon, Bill Keith, Tony Trischka, Pete Wernick, Noam Pikelny, and Jayme Stone among others.

He has performed and recorded extensively with many artists and bands, always on the folk scene but also in a wide range of styles, from flamenco to pop and rock music; he has also recorded original music for several films and CDs and performed on the theater stage as a musician/actor.

Widely acknowledged as a performer both at home and abroad, Lluís Gómez is one of the great connoisseurs of bluegrass music in Spain. He has written several methods for learning how to play the five-string banjo, including a bilingual Spanish-Catalan book written in collaboration with Toni Giménez. He regularly writes for several music-related magazines and in March 2015, he was featured on the cover of the prestigious *Banjo Newsletter* magazine.

He also plays mandolin and violin and is the co-author with Oriol Saña of a book called *The Bluegrass Violin* written in English and Spanish. He is also the author of *Fun Solos to Play, Early Classic Gems* and *Christmas in the British Isles*, all published by Mel Bay Publications. He runs the Bluegrass and Old-Time Music Festival *Al Ras* as well as the Barcelona Bluegrass Camp, and also teaches abroad at the prestigious International Stage Musique Acoustique Campus in Belgium.

He currently teaches banjo, mandolin and violin at various schools and plays in several bluegrass, folk, and jazz manouche bands, hosts a bluegrass session in Barcelona, and regularly contributes to different media.

Other Mel Bay Banjo Books